W9-BTF-120

REVIEW COPY
COURTESY OF
ENSLOW PUBLISHERS, IN

Courageous Heroes
of the American West

Sacagawea
Courageous
American Indian Guide

William R. Sanford and Carl R. Green

Enslow Publishers, Inc.
40 Industrial Road
Box 398
Berkeley Heights, NJ 07922
USA
http://www.enslow.com

Copyright © 2013 by William R. Sanford and Carl R. Green

All rights reserved.

No part of this book may be reproduced by any means
without the written permission of the Publisher.

Original edition published as *Sacagawea: Native American Hero* in 1997.

Library of Congress Cataloging-in-Publication Data

Sanford, William R. (William Reynolds), 1927–
    Sacagawea : courageous American Indian guide / William R. Sanford and Carl R. Green.
        p. cm. — (Courageous heroes of the American West)
    Includes index.
    Summary: "Discusses the life of Sacagawea, including her Shoshone childhood, her kidnapping
by the Hidatsa, her journey with the Lewis and Clark expedition, and her legacy in American
history"—Provided by publisher.
    ISBN 978-0-7660-4006-9
    1. Sacagawea—Juvenile literature. 2. Lewis and Clark Expedition (1804–1806)—Juvenile
literature. 3. Shoshoni women—Biography—Juvenile literature. 4. Shoshoni Indians—
Biography—Juvenile literature. I. Green, Carl R. II. Title.
    F592.7.S123S468 2013
    978.004'974574092—dc23
    [B]   2011048291

Future editions:
Paperback ISBN 978-1-4644-0096-4
ePUB ISBN 978-1-4645-1003-8
PDF ISBN 978-1-4646-1003-5

Printed in the United States of America
032012 Lake Book Manufacturing, Inc., Melrose Park, IL
10 9 8 7 6 5 4 3 2 1

To Our Readers: We have done our best to make sure all Internet addresses in this book were active
and appropriate when we went to press. However, the author and the Publisher have no control over,
and assume no liability for, the material available on those Internet sites or on other Web sites they
may link to. Any comments or suggestions can be sent by e-mail to comments@enslow.com or to the
address on the back cover.

♻ Enslow Publishers, Inc., is committed to printing our books on recycled paper. The paper in
every book contains 10% to 30% post-consumer waste (PCW). The cover board on the outside
of each book contains 100% PCW. Our goal is to do our part to help young people and the
environment too!

Illustration Credits: © 2011 Clipart.com, a division of Getty Images, p. 37; Enslow Publishers,
Inc., p. 25; © Enslow Publishers, Inc. / Paul Daly, p. 1; The Granger Collection, NYC, pp. 16, 33;
Independence National Historical Park, pp. 20, 21; John Kropewnicki / © 2011 Photos.com, a
division of Getty Images, p. 22; Keith Crowley / © 2011 Photos.com, a division of Getty Images,
p. 29; Library of Congress Prints and Photographs, p. 15; © Marilyn Angel Wynn / nativestock.com,
p. 7; © 2011 Photos.com, a division of Getty Images, p. 11; Shutterstock.com, p. 41; United States
coin image from the United States Mint, p. 42.

Cover Illustration: © Enslow Publishers, Inc. / Paul Daly.

Contents

Authors' Note

In 1804, President Thomas Jefferson ordered Meriwether Lewis and William Clark to explore the American Northwest. On their way west, the explorers hired guides and interpreters. One was a French fur trader named Toussaint Charbonneau. Lewis and Clark also obtained the services of Sacagawea, Charbonneau's young American Indian wife. It is this brave and resourceful young Shoshone woman who is most likely to capture our attention today.

Some writers have given Sacagawea credit for guiding Lewis and Clark to the Pacific coast. That was impossible. She had never been west of the Rocky Mountains. Sacagawea did serve as a guide and translator while traveling through regions she knew. Further, when Lewis and Clark met American Indian tribes, her presence helped prove that the white men came in peace. These contributions, combined with her wilderness skills, made her a valued member of the expedition.

In many books, writers spell Sacagawea's name with a "j"—Sacajawea. In this book, the authors spell her name with a "g." This is the spelling that Lewis and Clark used when writing their journals. However her name is spelled, you are about to read Sacagawea's true story. It is based on the expedition's journals and on American Indian oral histories.

Chapter 1

A Joyful Reunion

In 1805, the United States was looking westward. Two years earlier, President Thomas Jefferson had purchased the Louisiana Territory. The new nation now stretched from the Mississippi River to the Rocky Mountains. Captains Meriwether Lewis and William Clark were pushing deep into the Northwest. Their goal was to open a route to the Pacific.

On August 17, the Corps of Discovery was fifteen months out of St. Louis. It was a crucial time. The Rocky Mountains loomed ahead. Soon, their canoes would be useless. Lewis and Clark needed horses. The Shoshone were nearby—and the tribe bred fine horses.

Each American Indian tribe raised a new challenge. Some chiefs welcomed the white men. Others treated them as enemies. The captains had less reason to fear the Shoshone than the other tribes. Traveling with them was a Shoshone woman named Sacagawea. Taken captive as a child, she had grown up in a Hidatsa village to the east.

Sacagawea's husband, Toussaint Charbonneau, served as an interpreter. He did not speak Shoshone. Lewis and Clark were counting on the young wife and mother to interpret for them. That morning, she was picking berries near the Beaverhead River. Pomp, her infant son, rode in a cradleboard on her back.

All at once, Sacagawea spotted several Shoshone on horseback. The sight caused her to dance for joy. Turning, she put her fingers in her mouth. Clark read the gesture as meaning the riders were from her tribe. Astonished by her return, the Shoshone led the explorers to their camp. One of the white men described the meeting. As the party neared the camp, "a woman made her way through the crowd toward Sacagawea. . . . Recognizing each other, they embraced with the most tender affection. They had been companions in childhood." Like Sacagawea, Willow Woman had been taken captive—but she escaped and found her way home.

That afternoon, the American captains met with Chief Cameahwait. A sail from one of the dugout canoes shaded the men from the sun. The chief seated Clark on a white robe. Then he tied six small shells in Clark's red hair. As a further sign that the two groups met in peace, the men took off their moccasins. A sacred peace pipe passed from hand to hand.

In this illustration, Sacagawea poses with her son Pomp resting in a cradleboard at her side. When the Lewis and Clark expedition reached the Beaverhead River, Sacagawea met several Shoshone on horseback. Her reunion with her people was a joyous occasion for the young Shoshone woman.

Now it was time to talk. Lewis sent for Sacagawea to interpret. Without her, the council could not proceed. She entered the circle with her eyes cast down as a mark of respect for the tribe's elders. When the captains spoke, Charbonneau repeated their words in Hidatsa. Sacagawea then translated their comments into Shoshone.

Sacagawea sat near Clark, who made a speech that explained the purpose of his journey. Sacagawea looked up—and recognized the chief. Cameahwait was her older brother! She jumped up and threw her blanket around him. Then she wept as she hugged him. Brother and sister talked briefly. Sacagawea's tears of joy flowed freely as she returned to her seat.

Later, Sacagawea's happiness turned to sorrow. Most of her family had died. Only Cameahwait and her sister's son had survived. As custom required, she adopted the boy. Then she gave him to his uncles to be raised. At that point, an older warrior stepped forward. Sacagawea's father, the man claimed, had given her to him in marriage. He dropped his claim when he learned that Pomp was Charbonneau's child.

With Sacagawea's help, Lewis and Clark bought a string of packhorses. On August 27, they gave the command to move out. Sacagawea said farewell to her brother. She never saw him again.

Chapter 2

A Shoshone Childhood

Sacagawea's adventurous life began in Idaho's Lemhi River valley. Her father was a chief of the Shoshone. The tribal name means "People who live in the valley." Her year of birth was 1788. No one knows the day or month. It may have been in March, the Moon of the Rushing Waters.

It was common for American Indians to have more than one name during their lifetimes. Sacagawea's name at birth was Bo-i-naiv (Grass Maiden). The Hidatsa renamed her Sacagawea. That was the name Lewis and Clark knew her by. It translates as Bird Woman. In later years, she may have also been called Lost Woman, Porivo (Chief), and Water White-Man.

The Shoshone wandered north from Mexico hundreds of years before Sacagawea was born. For a time, the tribe lived in the Great Basin between the

Sierra Nevada and the Rocky Mountains. Then came a searing drought. As game animals left the basin, the Shoshone became nomads. Always on the move, they ate salmon, squirrels, rabbits, rats, and lizards. The children gathered roots, seeds, and berries. When hunters came home with empty hands, the women roasted crickets and grasshoppers. Water was scarce. Little could be spared for bathing.

In summer, the Shoshone dressed lightly. Men wore a breechcloth of badger hide. Women wore a leather apron. Men and women walked the rocky trails in yucca fiber sandals. Their homes were crude brush shelters called wickiups. When winter swept the basin, the Shoshone put on leggings, moccasins, and rabbit-fur capes.

By the late 1700s, some Shoshone bands had moved into the mountains. Sacagawea's people were one of these Plateau tribes. Fur traders who found them living near the Snake River called them the Snake people. The climate was harsh, however, there was water and game. Shoshone hunters killed deer, bear, sheep, beavers, and ducks with arrows and spears. Buckskin shirts and tunics became common. In time, some of the Shoshone found their way

This animal skin painting depicts a Shoshone buffalo hunt. The Shoshone moved east to the Great Plains because the hunting was better there. Buffalo provided a plentiful source of food, and the Shoshone used the hides for their tipis.

eastward to the Great Plains. The hunting was better there. One buffalo could feed an entire band.

Buffalo hunts brought the Shoshone into contact with the Plains tribes. With no common language, the hunters talked in sign language. The Shoshone way of life began to change. Wickiups gave way to tipis made of buffalo hides stretched over wooden poles. When the tribe moved, the people dragged their tipis with them. By the 1740s, the Shoshone were trading beaver pelts for handsome spotted horses. Hunters ranged far out on the plains in search of buffalo.

This was the world that Sacagawea knew as a child. Her brothers were trained to be hunters and warriors. She and her sisters were taught to gather food, cook, sew, and care for babies. Sacagawea learned how to gather and prepare over a hundred edible plants. One of her favorites was the camas lily. The Shoshone dried the potatolike bulbs and ate them.

Sacagawea's mother showed her how to cook a favorite dish. She used flat stones to grind acorns, nuts, and seeds into meal. Then she filled a large yucca basket with water, meal, and chunks of meat. A coating of pitch made the basket waterproof. To cook the stew, Sacagawea dropped hot stones from the campfire into the basket. The family ate the thick, tasty stew by dipping their fingers into the basket.

The Shoshone hunted buffalo with bows and arrows. Some rival Plains tribes had traded with white men for rifles. As the Shoshone pushed into their hunting grounds, these tribes pushed back. Peaceful contacts gave way to bloody hit-and-run raids. It was one of these violent raids that changed the course of Sacagawea's life.

Chapter 3

Captured by Hidatsa Raiders

Sometime around 1800, Sacagawea's father called for a summer hunt. His plan was to join other Shoshone at the three forks of the Missouri River in present-day western Montana. All the children knew the importance of the hunt. They would go hungry that winter if it failed.

Sacagawea rose at dawn with the rest of the band. The first job was to pack the family's belongings. Busy hands folded the tipi's hides and poles into a V-shaped frame. Called a travois, the frame was tied behind a horse and loaded with bundles. For the next three days, the twelve-year-old girl walked beside the heavily loaded travois. Only the men rode horseback.

The land of the three forks made a fine campsite. Snowcapped peaks towered over the valley. Beyond lay the plains and the buffalo herds. It was a peaceful scene, but the Shoshone were watchful. They knew that the warlike Hidatsa might ride out of the east at any time. Raiders would be seeking more than just horses and scalps. They would try to steal women and children as well.

Sacagawea's band met old friends at the forks. Lines of tipis soon dotted the riverbank. Scouts returned with word that buffalo were grazing nearby. The hunters mounted packhorses and galloped off. Each man led a second horse. These were the faster horses they used for the hunt.

That afternoon, Sacagawea's brother Cameahwait rode back with good news. The hunters had driven some buffalo over a cliff. Sacagawea and the other women hurried to the spot. First, they skinned the dead animals with sharp flint knives. Next, they hacked the flesh into smaller pieces and piled them on a travois. Horses dragged the meat and hides back to camp. That night, the Shoshone feasted on slabs of tender roast buffalo. The women cut the rest of the meat into strips. When laid in the sun, the strips would dry into a long-lasting food (today it is known as jerky). The dried meat was tough, but it was an essential part of the winter diet.

This Hidatsa warrior, dressed in ceremonial costume, prepares for a traditional dance. When Sacagawea accompanied her brother Cameahwait on a buffalo hunt, Hidatsa raiders attacked the Shoshone camp. During the raid, the warriors kidnapped Sacagawea.

In this George Catlin painting, traditional Hidatsa earth-covered lodges line a bluff above the Knife River in North Dakota. When her captors reached the Hidatsa village near present-day Bismarck, North Dakota, Sacagawea saw these unusual dwellings for the first time.

The women had to scrape the fat from the hides before they could be tanned. Sacagawea took her turn with the scraper the next morning. It was hot, tiring work. In the afternoon, she joined the other girls by the river. As they chatted, a burst of gunfire shattered the quiet. The girls saw a band of Hidatsa warriors riding into the camp. Most of the Shoshone men were out hunting. Those who were left knew their bows were no match for rifles. The men scattered. The women grabbed their children and fled.

Sacagawea tried to find a hiding place. A thick grove of trees on the other side of the river caught her eye. She ran into the river, the icy current tugging at her legs. Her feet slipped on the rocks. Behind her, a horse splashed into the river. A moment later, a strong arm plucked her from the water. Sacagawea struggled, but the warrior held her fast.

The Hidatsa fired at anything that moved. Four men, four women, and several boys soon lay dead or dying. As fruits of their success, the raiders carried off Shoshone horses and captives. Their route home followed the Yellowstone River, then the Missouri.

At times, Sacagawea's captor allowed her to ride. More often she and the other captives were forced to walk. Soon the mountains faded from sight. Blowing sand stung their faces. Only sagebrush and tumbleweeds grew in the gray alkaline soil. Farther east, a sea of prairie grass stretched to the horizon.

At last, the Hidatsa reached their village on the Knife River. The city of Bismarck, North Dakota, would one day be built on the site. Sacagawea had never before seen a village circled by a wall of logs. Inside the wall, the Hidatsa lived in round, earth-covered lodges. The gates swung open as the raiding party drew near. Tied to the back of a horse, Sacagawea rode toward an uncertain future.

Chapter 4

Forest Bear and Little Chief

Unlike the Shoshone, the Hidatsa were farmers as well as hunters. With crops to cultivate, they lived year-round in their villages. Inside each round lodge, the floor lay a foot or more below ground level. The step-down floors and thick walls kept the lodges cool in summer and warm in winter.

Sacagawea's captor, a man named Red Arrow, put her to work in the fields. Each day she tended the maize, squash, and beans. To hoe the maize, she used a tool made from a buffalo's shoulder bone. At harvest time, she stacked the ears on a platform to dry. Later, the Hidatsa beat the ears with sticks to free the kernels.

A year or two passed. Then, one winter's night, Sacagawea's life changed again. Like many Hidatsa men, Red Arrow liked to gamble. The game he played was simple. First, the players made their bets. Next, a "dealer" hid a pebble under one of four moccasins.

Guessing wrong cost the player his bet—a fur, some beads, or a knife. One night, Red Arrow lost a bet with Toussaint Charbonneau. Pulling Sacagawea to her feet, Red Arrow pushed her toward the French-Canadian fur trader. He had bet her against the trader's buffalo horse.

Charbonneau made Sacagawea his third wife. One of the older wives was a Hidatsa woman and the other a Shoshone named Otter Woman. Charbonneau was thirty years older than Sacagawea. The Hidatsa said he was slow-witted and clumsy. They called him Forest Bear. His fellow fur traders said he was a sneak and a scoundrel.

In the spring of 1804, Sacagawea became pregnant. As the months passed, she made fur-lined clothing for the baby. One day that fall, Charbonneau rushed in with amazing news. In Hidatsa, he told her that white men had been seen on the river.

Down at the riverbank, Sacagawea caught her first glimpse of the strangers. She stared at their pale skin and blue uniforms. In time, she met the two leaders. The blond silent man was Captain Meriwether Lewis, and the cheerful redhead was Captain William Clark. Clark never did learn how to pronounce Sacagawea's name. He called her Janey.

Sacagawea caught her first glimpse of the pale-skinned American explorers in the spring of 1804. Captain Meriwether Lewis is shown here in this portrait painted by Charles Willson Peale.

The explorers were sailing upriver in three boats. The largest was a keelboat with a cannon mounted at each end. The two smaller boats were canoe-shaped dugouts called pirogues. The white men landed and pitched tents near the river. A lively trading session followed. The Hidatsa and their Mandan neighbors bartered cornmeal and furs for medals and tobacco.

The chiefs allowed the captains to build a winter camp. Sacagawea marveled at the speed with which the soldiers' axes chopped down trees. A log fort soon rose on the site. Captains Lewis and Clark named it Fort Mandan. When they needed an interpreter, they hired Charbonneau.

William Clark never learned to properly pronounce Sacagawea's name, so he called her Janey. This Charles Willson Peale portrait shows the brave redheaded captain as he might have dressed for his wedding to Julia Hancock.

Village gossip told Sacagawea more about the white men. Their chief was President Thomas Jefferson. He had purchased a vast tract of land from a country called France. This Louisiana Territory included the lands of the Hidatsa and Mandan. Now Jefferson wanted to know more about the land. What grew there? Who lived there? Was there an easy route through the mountains to the great western sea?

Charbonneau saw a chance to make some money. He offered to accompany Lewis and Clark when they embarked to paddle up the Missouri in the spring. When they reached the land of the Shoshone, he and Sacagawea could interpret. It was a good argument.

The captains knew that they would have to trade for Shoshone horses when they left the river.

On February 11, 1805, Sacagawea gave birth to a son. A friend gave her a tonic to make the birth easier. The drink was made of crushed rattlesnake rattles. Charbonneau named the boy Jean Baptiste. Clark nicknamed the baby "Pomp." In Shoshone, the nickname meant First Born, or Little Chief.

By March, Sacagawea was strong again. Pomp was thriving and the weather was good. The captains gave the orders to prepare for the trip westward.

This 1950s postage stamp pictured Sacagawea standing with Lewis and Clark. Behind them, crewmen prepare the boats used by the Corps of Discovery for the journey upriver.

Chapter 5

A Perilous Journey

On April 7, 1805, Lewis and Clark left Fort Mandan. Their party included twenty-seven soldiers, two interpreters, Sacagawea, and Pomp. All embarked in two pirogues and six small canoes. Lewis felt the thrill of heading into the unknown. In his journal, he compared his tiny fleet to the ships that Columbus sailed to the New World.

To escape the crowded pirogue, Sacagawea often trekked along the riverbanks. Walking gave her a chance to gather plants. Wild onions, berries, plums, and Jerusalem artichokes found their way onto the camp menu. At night, Sacagawea and Pomp shared the one tent with Charbonneau and the two captains.

The men survived dangerous run-ins with bears and rattlesnakes. But it was the river that caused the most trouble. On May 14, a wind gust tipped the lead pirogue on its side. The boat righted itself, but much of the cargo spilled out. As the men paddled for shore, Sacagawea calmly retrieved the floating bundles. Her quick thinking saved journals, scientific instruments, and medicines. A few days later, Lewis and Clark named a waterway in her honor. The stream they called Bird Woman's River is known today as Crooked Creek.

On June 10, Sacagawea fell ill. Puzzled by her symptoms, Clark tried bleeding her. Then he dosed her with laudanum and applied pine bark poultices. A check of her pulse led Lewis to fear for her life. He added mineral water to the treatment. The pungent drink seemed to help her. By June 17, his patient was sipping soup. On the day her appetite came back, she ate too many green apples. That night, the pain and fever returned. Lewis scolded Charbonneau for not taking care of her. By the next day, however, Sacagawea felt well enough to go fishing.

The next near disaster struck a few days later. To escape a severe hailstorm, Clark led Sacagawea and Pomp to shelter under a rock ledge. All at once, a wall of water surged through the canyon. Sacagawea grabbed Pomp just as the flash flood carried off his cradleboard. Clark then pushed mother and son up the steep hillside to safety.

With Pomp on her back, Sacagawea gamely forged ahead with Lewis and Clark, overcoming illness and nature's challenges. This map shows the route taken by the Corps of Discovery as it headed up the Missouri River on its way to the Pacific Coast.

One day, Sacagawea saw trees that had been stripped of their edible bark. It was a sign that she was nearing the land of the Shoshone. In July, she found the spot where she had been captured. Two weeks later, she danced for joy to see her people again.

Riding Shoshone horses over Shoshone land, the explorers pushed westward. The Lolo Trail led them into the land of the Nez Percé. At first, the Nez Percé feared that the white men would attack them. The sight of Sacagawea and Pomp eased their fears. War parties, they knew, did not travel with women and children. The tribe fed the strangers and provided guides.

The expedition crossed the Great Divide in knee-deep snow. Next came the Clearwater River. This was a milestone. Rivers now flowed west instead of east. The Nez Percé guides described a river route that followed the Clearwater to the Snake. The Snake, in turn, flowed into the Columbia. It was the Columbia that would carry them to the sea. Before heading west in dugout canoes, the men buried their extra supplies. The Nez Percé promised to care for the horses.

In October, Lewis and Clark headed their canoes downriver. Food was scarce. The men butchered dogs and horses for food. Tribal custom kept Sacagawea from eating the meat. She lived on fish, plants, and roots until Lewis bagged some ducks.

The Columbia came into view on October 16. Lewis and Clark hoped for an easy passage, but the great river defied them. The men had to carry their canoes and supplies around rapids and waterfalls. Rain fell almost daily. Clothing and bedding rotted.

On November 7, Sacagawea heard the roar of breaking waves. The explorers were certain that they had reached the ocean. "O the joy!" Clark wrote. "The cheering view exhilarated the spirits of all the party."

Chapter 6

A Dreary Winter on the Pacific Coast

The explorers soon discovered their mistake. What looked like the ocean was only the wide mouth of the Columbia. Sacagawea and some of the men became seasick as waves tossed the canoes. Lewis and Clark beached the canoes at Point Ellice, twenty miles from the ocean. Fog and rain further dampened the men's spirits. They lived on dried fish and roots supplied by the local Chinook tribe.

Clark wanted to go upriver to find a dry campsite. Lewis argued that they should spend the winter on the coast. If a ship came by, he wanted to buy medicines and other supplies. They might even book passage and sail home in comfort.

Scouts found good hunting on the south side of the river. On December 5, Lewis picked a site a few miles inland for a winter camp. The spot lay on high ground amid a grove of tall fir trees. A spring flowed nearby. Sacagawea voted with the others to approve the choice. Anxious to escape the rain, the men started work on Fort Clatsop. The name paid tribute to people from the Clatsop tribe who brought gifts of food.

Eight cabins with sloping roofs rose on the site. Douglas firs yielded fine boards two feet in width. Work crews also salvaged lumber from an old Chinook village. A stout log stockade completed the defenses. On Christmas Eve, Sacagawea, Charbonneau, and Pomp moved into a room of their own.

The men observed Christmas with songs and a loud chorus of rifle fire. Sacagawea gave Clark two dozen white weasel tails. The Shoshone prized the tails for their beauty. The Christmas feast featured elk meat (spoiled) and roast wapato roots (delicious). Sacagawea was fond of this potato-like food.

By the next day, the men were back at work. There was furniture to build and clothing to mend. Hunting parties tracked and bagged elk, deer, beaver, and sea otter. Sacagawea helped sew moccasins and shirts from the hides. By boiling seawater, the men made four quarts of "white, fine" salt a day. The cooks used the salt for flavoring and to preserve meat.

To escape the rains that pelted the Corps of Discovery when it reached the Pacific Coast, the men built Fort Clatsop. Sacagawea, Charbonneau, and Pomp were given their own room. This photo shows a reconstruction of the stockade and log walls

The constant rain shrouded the fort in gloom. The men suffered from colds, flu, boils, and lumbago. Fleas infested the camp. Sentries stood guard to keep the Chinook from stealing tools and supplies. Lewis and Clark preferred the Clatsop. Sacagawea spoke in sign language to Chief Comowoll when he came to trade.

On January 5, the Clatsop brought news of a beached whale. As Clark made plans to visit the site, Sacagawea asked for a favor. Lewis reported her request in these words: "The poor woman stated . . .

that she had traveled a great way with us to see the great water, yet she had never been down to the coast. Now that this monstrous fish was also to be seen, it seemed hard that she should be permitted to see neither the ocean nor the whale."

Two days later, Sacagawea stood on a bluff above the Pacific. The "great water" looked as though it stretched to the edge of the world. She lifted eleven-month-old Pomp so he could see waves crash on the sand. By that time, the Clatsop had stripped the great "fish" of blubber. When Sacagawea reached the beach, she marveled at the immense bones. Clark measured the whale's length at 105 feet.

As the weeks passed, hopes of meeting a supply ship died. Lewis and Clark worked on their notes and planned the return trip. Lewis traded his gold-laced coat for a canoe. As a good-bye gift, the captains gave Fort Clatsop to Chief Comowoll.

The skies finally cleared at midday on March 23, 1806. Sacagawea took a seat in one of the canoes. The dug-outs moved slowly up the river as the men bent to their paddles.

Chapter 7

The Return Trip

T he hunting was good along the Columbia that spring of 1806. By early April, the party had salted down a good supply of meat. Most of the American Indians the explorers met were friendly. A few turned out to be thieves. Lewis had to send three armed men to recover his guard dog, Seaman.

Swift currents forced Lewis and Clark to abandon their canoes. Once again, they needed horses, and Sacagawea helped buy them. This time the Walla Walla tribe furnished the packhorses. To prove his friendship, Chief Yellept gave Clark a fine white horse. Clark, not to be outdone, gave Yellept his sword.

The expedition reached the Nez Percé in early May. In one village, an old man said that the white men had come to kill his people. Sacagawea found a visiting Shoshone who spoke the Nez Percé language.

Through him, she convinced the chiefs that Lewis and Clark had come in peace. Clark further won the tribe's trust with his self-taught doctoring skills. He treated wounds, set broken bones, and rinsed irritated eyes.

Clark's skills were sorely tested by Pomp's illness late in May. At almost fourteen months, Pomp was cutting teeth. To add to his discomfort, he developed a high fever, a swollen neck, and diarrhea. The two captains worried about him. Lewis wrote on May 24: "The child was very wrestless [sic] last night. [Its] jaw and the back of [its] neck are much more swol[l]en than they were yesterday." Clark treated the diarrhea with cream of tartar. Then he applied a poultice of hot onions to the boy's neck. Later, he switched to a salve made of pine resin, beeswax, and bear's oil. By early June, Pomp was his happy self again.

The men's all-meat diet left them with headaches and stomachaches. Sacagawea's knowledge of wild plants helped relieve the symptoms. A trip through the woods produced fennel (a carrotlike root) and wild onions. The flavor of the horse and dog stew improved and so did the men's health.

Lewis and Clark split the party after crossing the Rockies. Lewis turned north, hoping to find a shorter route to the Great Falls. Clark headed south along the

William Clark sketched this sage grouse in his journal, along with comments he transcribed from Meriwether Lewis. During the expedition, the two explorers kept detailed journals, often drawing maps, recording observations, and illustrating new discoveries.

Yellowstone River. The plan called for them to meet where the Yellowstone joins the Missouri. Sacagawea, Pomp, and Charbonneau went with Clark.

For a time, Clark followed a well-traveled trail. All went well until he reached the plains. There the trail branched in many directions. Sacagawea stepped forward. Her people once had come here to dig camas roots, she said. She told Clark to head for the highest part of the plain. From there, he would see a gap in the mountains. Crossing that gap, she promised, would lead them to where their supplies were hidden.

Clark followed her advice. On July 8, the party reached the Jefferson River and the cache of supplies. A few days later, Sacagawea again pointed the way. As they neared the Yellowstone River, Clark saw two passes ahead. He wrote: "[Sacagawea] has been of great service to me as a pilot through this country. [She] recommends a gap in the mountains more south which I shall cross." Today, that gap is known as the Bozeman Pass.

The weather was cold enough to leave a film of ice on standing water. It was not cold enough to drive off the mosquitoes. Swarms of the pesky insects sometimes kept hunters from aiming their rifles. On the south side of the Yellowstone, Clark climbed a two-hundred-foot pillar of rock. With little Pomp in mind, he named it Pompy's Tower. Today it is known as Pompey's Pillar.

Clark and his party met Lewis and his men two weeks later. Now it was time for the party to paddle down the Missouri. On August 14, 1806, they sighted a Mandan village. Crowds turned out to watch their progress. Soon, the Hidatsa villages came into view. Sacagawea was home again.

Chapter 8

Homecoming

No record exists of Sacagawea's homecoming. We can guess that the women treated her with respect. She had been little more than a girl when she left. Now, eighteen months later, she returned a strong, confident woman. Her baby had grown into an active, handsome child. Most of all, Sacagawea had played a major role in the expedition's success.

Clark had grown quite fond of Pomp. He wrote: "I offered to take [her] little son, a beautiful promising child who is 19 months old." The offer was well meant, but Pomp had not been weaned. Charbonneau asked Clark to wait a year. Clark agreed and promised to raise Pomp in "such a manner as I thought proper."

Fire had destroyed Fort Mandan. Lewis and Clark set up camp near a Mandan village. The captains urged the Mandan and Hidatsa chiefs to visit St. Louis. But in the end, only one chief agreed. The others feared the passage through the lands of the Sioux. Their refusal meant that Charbonneau was no longer needed to interpret.

Clark gave Charbonneau $500. The money paid for his services as an interpreter and for his horse and tent. If Sacagawea received any pay, it was not recorded. Clark did pay her tribute in his journal. "[Sacagawea] was particularly useful among the Shoshone. Indeed, she had borne with a patience truly admirable the fatigues of so long a route encumbered with the charge of an infant."

Three days later, the captains said their good-byes and headed downstream. On August 20, Clark wrote to Sacagawea and Charbonneau. His letter renewed his offer to raise Pomp. He called the child his "little dancing boy." Clark added, "If you wish to live with the white people, and will come to me, I will give you a piece of land . . . horses, cows and hogs."

That fall, Charbonneau took Sacagawea and Pomp to St. Louis. He also brought along Otter Woman, his second Shoshone wife. She was older than Sacagawea, and her son, Toussaint, was older than little Pomp. Charbonneau spent the next few years in the woods.

In this illustration, Sacagawea directs Lewis and Clark during the trek westward. When the Corps of Discovery returned home, Sacagawea did not receive any money for her contributions during the journey, but Clark did pay tribute to her in his journal.

In October 1810, he bought the farmland Clark had offered him. A few months later, he sold the land back to Clark for $100. The fur trader had tired quickly of life as a farmer.

In 1811, Charbonneau traveled upriver with a lawyer named Henry Brackenridge. The fur trader had only one of his wives with him. He left his sons behind in St. Louis, where Clark acted as their guardian.

Meriwether Lewis had died in 1809. Clark was carving out a new career as Superintendent of Indian Affairs.

Brackenridge wrote: "We have on board a Frenchman named Chabonet [sic], with his wife . . . both of whom accompanied Lewis and Clark to the Pacific. . . . The woman [is] a good creature of mild and gentle disposition. [She] was greatly attracted to whites, whose manners and airs she tries to imitate. . . . She longed to revisit her native country." As often happened when whites wrote about American Indian women, he did not use Sacagawea's name.

War with Great Britain broke out in the spring of 1812. The threat from Canada alarmed a rich fur trader named Manuel Lisa. The wealthy trader ordered his men to build Fort Manuel on the northern border of South Dakota. Charbonneau was part of the work crew. John Luttig was one of the clerks.

On December 20, Luttig wrote: "This evening the wife of Charbonneau . . . died of a putrid fever. She was . . . the best woman in the fort, aged about 25 years. She left a fine infant girl."

Luttig did not record the name of the woman who died. When Clark read the report, he assumed she was Sacagawea. Was this the end of the Bird Woman's story?

Chapter 9

A Lasting Legacy

As the nation moved westward, few stopped to think about Sacagawea. Decades passed before interest was reborn. In the 1920s, the Bureau of Indian Affairs sent Charles Eastman to look into the Bird Woman's life. Historian Grace Hebard used Eastman's report in her 1932 book, *Sacajawea*. Hebard and Eastman agreed that "the wife of Charbonneau" who died in 1812 was Otter Woman. Sacagawea, they claimed, lived another seventy-two years. The two historians developed a theory about Sacagawea's life after her supposed death in 1812.

Hebard and Eastman talked to people who had known the Bird Woman. Around 1820, they wrote, Charbonneau and Sacagawea were out west trapping beaver. Problems cropped up when Charbonneau wed a pretty Ute woman. Sacagawea disliked the new wife.

When the women quarreled, Charbonneau sided with his new wife. One day, he beat Sacagawea in front of her. It was not her first beating, but this time Sacagawea packed up and left. After months of wandering, she settled with the Comanche. Their language was a close kin to her native tongue.

Sacagawea soon married a Comanche. As the years passed, she gave birth to five more children. Only a son and a daughter survived. After her husband died in battle, Sacagawea decided to rejoin her own people. When she slipped away, her son Ticannaf led a fruitless search to find her. The Comanche began to call her Wadze-wipe, the Lost Woman.

No one knows what route Sacagawea took. She may have joined explorer John Charles Frémont's second expedition. In 1843, Frémont wrote: "An Indian woman of the Snake nation, desirous . . . to return to her people . . . obtained permission to travel with my party."

The woman, who was not named, left Frémont at Fort Bridger in Wyoming. Was she Sacagawea? The meeting with Frémont may be a clue. In that age, only a handful of American Indian women had the self-confidence to speak as equals with white men.

This statue of Sacagawea stands in Salmon, Idaho, the present-day town that grew up near her birthplace. Similar monuments can be found in a number of other states as well.

Sacagawea's travels in the years that followed are hard to pin down. One report has her moving from Canada to Arizona to California. The next evidence comes from the 1860s. During that decade, Sacagawea returned to Wyoming and the Shoshone. Her adopted son Bazil gave her a warm welcome. Government agents used her as an interpreter. Agent James Patten

In January 2000, the United States honored the heroic Shoshone woman by issuing the Sacagawea dollar. The gold-copper coin features her likeness, along with that of little Pomp.

was still living in 1926. He confirmed that Sacagawea lived with the Shoshone in the 1870s.

Sacagawea urged the tribe to take up farming. The buffalo, elk, and deer would soon be gone, she warned. When tribal councils met, Sacagawea's words carried great weight. At one council she urged a move to a reservation in the Wind River Mountains. Her people called her Porivo (Chief) because the whites showed her so much respect.

Sacagawea sometimes wore a medal Clark had given her. She liked to tell the story of the time she fed dog meat to hungry white men. Her great-grandson remembered her as "very old, but bright and gay." When she died, mourners wrapped her in skins. A favorite horse carried her body to the graveyard. Bazil put a small wooden marker at the site. When that vanished, the family marked the grave with small boulders. Today, a fine gravestone still stands guard. It reads:

SACAJAWEA
DIED APRIL 9, 1884
A GUIDE WITH THE
LEWIS AND CLARK
EXPEDITION
1805–1806

There still is no definitive proof about the actual date of Sacagawea's death. Although Hebard's theory was perpetuated further in many twentieth-century books, encyclopedias, and movies, the majority of historians now agree that Sacagawea did die on December 20, 1812, at Fort Manuel in South Dakota. Eight months after her death, Clark adopted Sacagawea's two children, Pomp and Lisette. Clark later provided for Pomp's education.

Despite the cloudy history surrounding her death, Sacagawea's legacy still lives on. There are more monuments dedicated to her than to any other American woman. Statues and markers can be found from St. Louis to Portland, Oregon. In Montana, Sacagawea Peak overlooks the rivers she traveled. Washington state is home to Sacajawea State Park and Lake Sacajawea. In January 2000, the United States Treasury began issuing the Sacagawea dollar, a coin featuring her likeness that was last minted in 2011. Each tribute adds to the legend of the brave Shoshone woman who helped blaze the trail west.

Glossary

bleeding—An outmoded medical technique that treated illness by draining blood from a patient's veins.

blubber—The thick layer of fat found between the skin and muscle layers of whales and other marine mammals.

breechcloth—An American Indian garment that covered the thighs and groin.

buckskins—Clothing made from the tanned hides of male deer.

Bureau of Indian Affairs—The government agency that tries to help American Indians make the best use of their land and resources.

cradleboard—A board or frame used by an American Indian mother to carry a baby on her back. Wrappings bound the baby tightly to the cradleboard.

flash flood—A sudden, powerful flood, usually caused by heavy rain.

Great Divide—A series of North American mountain ridges from which rivers flow westward on the western side and eastward on the eastern side.

interpreter—Someone who translates one language into a second language.

keelboat—A riverboat built for carrying freight. In Lewis and Clark's day, keelboats could be sailed, rowed, poled, or towed.

laudanum—A form of opium that was used as a painkiller in the 1800s.

lodge—A general name for a wilderness shelter.

maize—A type of corn raised by American Indians.

moccasins—The soft leather shoes made popular by American Indians.

peace pipe—A highly decorated pipe that American Indians used in their ceremonies.

pirogue—A large canoe made from a hollowed-out log.

pitch—A waterproof resin that American Indians obtained from pine trees.

poultice—A soft, moist cloth that is used to treat an aching or inflamed part of the body.

scalps—Portions of the skin and hair cut from human heads as battle trophies.

tipi—A portable dwelling used by some American Indians.

travois—A cargo-carrying frame slung between trailing poles and pulled by a dog or horse.

weaning—The process of training a baby to take nourishment other than by suckling.

wickiup—A frame hut covered with bark or brush.

yucca—A stiff-leaved, stemless succulent, native to Mexico and the western United States.

Further Reading

Books

Berne, Emma Carlson. *Sacagawea: Crossing the Continent With Lewis & Clark*. New York: Sterling, 2010.

Crosby, Michael T. *Sacagawea: Lewis & Clark's Pathfinder*. Stockton, N.J.: OTTN Publishing, 2007.

Gondosch, Linda. *Where Did Sacagawea Join the Corps of Discovery?: And Other Questions About the Lewis and Clark Expedition*. Minneapolis, Minn.: Lerner Publishing Group, 2011.

Nelson, Maria. *The Life of Sacagawea*. New York: Gareth Stevens Publishing, 2012.

Perritano, John. *The Lewis and Clark Expedition*. New York: Children's Press, 2010.

Internet Addresses

Lewis and Clark—Inside the Corps: Sacagawea
<http://www.pbs.org/lewisandclark/inside/saca.html>

National Geographic: Sacagawea
<http://ngm.nationalgeographic.com/ngm/0302/feature4/>

Sacagawea: Lewis and Clark Trail
<http://lewisandclarktrail.com/sacajawea.htm>

Index